Reflections
of a
Cape Cod Washashore

by

Ken Brynildsen

Enjoy !
Ken Brynildsen

INKLINGS PUBLISHING   Sandwich, Massachusetts 02563

PUBLISHING HISTORY

First published in 1997 by INKLINGS PUBLISHING
8 Bridle Path Circle
Sandwich, Massachusetts 02563
Phone: (508)888-7854
Fax: (508)888-6212

ISBN 0-9659205-1-8

Cover photo by the author.

Acknowledgments

The following essays first appeared in the <u>New York Times</u> in 1989 and 1990: <u>The Window</u>, <u>Parent's Weekend</u>, <u>My Two Fathers</u>, <u>A Lost Tooth</u>, <u>My College Car</u>. In addition, <u>Parent's Weekend</u> and <u>The Window</u> appeared in <u>Sunshine Magazine</u> in 1989.

***

There are so many people to whom I owe thanks for the encouragement they offered—and continue to offer—in regards to my writing. First, of course, is my wife, Linda. I can't imagine my life without her as my partner. And then my daughter, Shereen, and my son, Jesse. How does a father thank his children for the love and respect they so willingly give? Maybe by giving back the same kind of love and respect. . . God knows, they deserve it.

And of the many fine teachers I've had over the years, I'd like to thank two here. First is Catherine Parsell, the first teacher to make me believe that what I wrote was worth reading. The second is Harriet Sobol, an excellent teacher and wonderful friend who guided me through my initial steps as a professional writer. I'd also like to thank one of my many friends here, a fellow pilgrim of the pen, Paul Levine.

I am blessed to have each of you in my life.

Dedicated to

Linda, Shereen and Jesse;
three of my life's most treasured blessings.

Contents

1

A Lost Tooth

Awhile back, my son lost a tooth, and I lost my temper. Actually, it happened the other way around. First, I lost my temper, and then the tooth came out.

My son's baby teeth arrived late. The first one didn't show up until he was nearly a year old. His permanent teeth seem to be following suit. He's been disarming people with his freckled-faced, toothless grin now for more than 18 months. My wife's been so anxious about his top front teeth that she had his head x-rayed at the dentist just to make sure the teeth were there.

They *are* there, and they are BIG. In fact, it was the slow descent of these skateboards that led to the confrontation between my son and me.

One of these new teeth dislodged one of his baby teeth as insistently as a bulldozer uproots a tree. The displaced tooth remained, wobbling in his gum. That's when the trouble started. My son doesn't take kindly to losing things, particularly pieces of his body. Since his teeth are pieces of his body, the imminent loss of this tooth led to a scene.

I can't say I blame him for being upset. Whenever I lose one of *my* teeth, I consider it a mile marker along my tortuous route to the grave.

But it wasn't my son's anguish I had trouble dealing with. It was his complete surrender to that anguish.

This isn't just an example of misplaced male ego on my part. After having lost a number of my own teeth—as well as a lot of other things in life—I've come to believe that if one sur-

1

renders completely to pain, then eventually one surrenders completely to the fear of pain, and finally, one simply surrenders to fear itself.

I'm not one of those fools who denies the existence of pain when I'm feeling it. Nor do I deny fear when it rears its ugly head. But I try not to give in completely to either. I've found that if I can retain a modicum of control, I can maintain my sense of balance. And it's balance that keeps me from tumbling into the abyss of chaos.

Chaos was right where my son was headed as his big tooth bullied his little tooth loose from its mooring. He wouldn't eat, and he spoke as though his mouth were full of marbles. He couldn't concentrate in school, and he couldn't even enjoy play.

When I offered to help him remove the tooth, thereby ending his torment, he grew hysterical, fearing I'd ignore his right to work it free himself by demanding to remove it in my own way.

Frustrated and angry, I told him he was acting like a baby, and that I was ashamed of his lack of control. I told him that pain, like joy, was a part of life and that he damned well better face the fact and deal with it better than he was dealing with his loose tooth. Having heaped these adult admonitions on his young ego, I abandoned him, weeping, at the kitchen table.

As I sat in my office at the other end of the house, I tried to convince myself that I was right. Pain *is* a part of life. Surrendering all self-control *does* make things worse. Knowing this, why was I feeling so guilty? If I was right, why did I feel so wrong? Then it hit me. I had just surrendered to my anger as completely as he'd surrendered to his fear. Now, we each sat alone, dealing with our shame.

Before I'd mustered enough courage to go to him and apologize, he quietly stepped into my office. His eyes were red and his cheeks were smudged from crying. "Would you help me, dad?" he said, struggling to control his voice. "I need someone who knows what he's doing. Would you help me get the tooth out?"

"Sure," I said, struggling now to control my own voice. "You push from the back with your tongue, and I'll push gently from the front with my thumb."

2

The tooth came out in three seconds with a subtle *snap*.

"Is it bleeding?" His eyes teetered on the edge of panic.

I shook my head. "Hardly at all."

His relief was immediate. His posture improved. He went on and on about how he couldn't believe it was over so quickly. I told him how proud of him I felt and how brave he'd been to come to me after rejecting my help earlier. The marbles disappeared from his speech, and he went out to ride his scooter after instructing me to leave the tooth under his pillow for the tooth fairy.

I sat in my chair and watched him through the bay window. Then I gazed down at the little tooth in my hand. I thought of how long it had taken to appear in his mouth. I thought of how well it had served him over the years. Now it lay in my palm, a useless pebble soon to be cast away and lost forever in the nether world of tooth fairydom.

I headed upstairs, went into his room, and tucked the tooth under his pillow. I wondered if the tooth fairy would know how much had been lost and how much had been gained through this little tooth. Would she know that a little boy had learned to rise above his fear in making room for a bigger and better tooth? Would she know a father had learned that keeping his balance depended as much on controlling his anger as it did on controlling his fear?

Yes, the tooth fairy would know these things. I guess she knows just about everything there is to know about little boys, teeth and the impatience of fathers.

2
The Window

I came down out of the trees to join corporate America. I mean that quite literally. I was a tree surgeon for nearly two decades before I dropped into a Fortune 100 company in 1981. Being a young tree surgeon was just fine. Every day was different. Some days were terribly frightening. Some days were beautiful beyond description. I didn't need to listen to weather reports. Unlike contemporary meteorologists, I lived every day in the weather. Like the furred and feathered critters with whom I shared the trees, I was intimate with the seasons— always aware of what was in the wind.

Being a middle-aged tree surgeon was not fine. Recovering from a hard day's work took too much time. Even hung over, the younger ones were faster than I. Stronger too. I could still outwork them, or at least keep up, because of what I knew. But how long would *that* last?

I married and had children. I didn't want to build my nest in a tree, so with both feet on the ground, I accepted a position in a major corporation. I was hired onto a third-shift manufacturing line that produced computer chips. I gave up my climbing saddle and hand saw for alignment tools and ion implanters.

For a long time, I didn't miss working outside. The vision of working outdoors for most people who have never done it is more romantic than realistic. With the exception of two months (three in a good year), the weather's either too hot, too cold or too wet to be comfortable. I felt grateful to be locked away in the warm, dry womb of the plant. I didn't even sit near the windows in the cafeteria at lunch time. Then again, lunch for third-shifters is at 4 a.m., and there's not much to see at that hour even if one *does* sit near the window.

There were no windows in our work area. We worked in clean rooms, wearing white hoods and lime-green, floor-length smocks. The women weren't allowed to wear makeup because of potential product contamination. It didn't matter anyway. With or without makeup, we all looked like tubes of tooth paste. Some tubes fuller than others.

Through a series of fortunate circumstances and hard work on my part, I was moved off the third shift line and into a day job, wearing tie and jacket. I moved my stuff out of my locker and into my desk. I'd arrived. I had my own office. Without a window.

As the months passed, my walks to the window at the far end of the hallway became more frequent. I found myself standing and gazing for longer and longer periods at the unspoiled hills beyond the parking lot. I watched through the glass as the trees changed colors with the seasons. I'd close my eyes and easily recall the feel of different tree barks against my palms. The smoothness of beech, the stiff roughness of hickory. With my eyes closed, I could feel the velvety warmth of a sun-touched magnolia petal. I could smell the fragrance of May's purple lilacs.

I hung pictures on my walls. They were shots of outdoor scenes I'd taken on my cross-country adventures of years before. Like a key, each picture unlocked a memory of how I'd felt at the time. Colleagues would stop by my office, gaze at the pictures and reminisce about memories the pictures evoked in them.

Over the years, my offices changed. The walls changed. Sometimes they got closer. Sometimes they moved farther apart. But never was a wall interrupted by a window. No matter where I was moved to, I found a window. Often it was at the end of a hallway. Sometimes it was tucked away in a little alcove. Those were the ones I loved the best, because I could linger there longer without being seen and judged undisciplined by my superiors.

In time, I grew to understand that only high-ranking individuals were granted offices with windows. Only when you proved to the higher powers that you were self-disciplined and too dedicated to your work to waste time gazing out a window were you granted a window. There were only so many windows available. They were granted to those who wouldn't misuse them.

I remember one fall day in particular. I knew it was fall, not by the puffy, white clouds scudding across the brilliant blue sky outside the window, but because my desk calendar said it was a day in October. As I stood, gazing out the window, a flock of Canada geese flew by. They unearthed a memory of another flock of geese I'd seen many years before.

At the time, I was sixty feet up in a beech tree. The top of the tree was dead and had to come out. It was a dangerous job. Supporting cables below me, cables that held together the massive leaders of the tree, had rusted through and snapped. The limbs to be removed had to be lowered to avoid damaging the roof of the house below me. An inexperienced ground man was handling the lowering lines. A wrong move on either of our parts could result in disaster. Suddenly, I heard a strange whooshing sound behind me. It raised the hackles on my neck. It approached so quickly that I didn't have time to turn and see what it was before it was right on top of me. It was a flock of geese. As they soared by, their wings beating through the air, they started honking. For a split second, I felt as though I was a member of the flock. In the next split second, I knew that I no longer belonged in the trees. It was the last tree I climbed.

As I gazed through the window at this new flock of geese, I suddenly realized that I couldn't hear them. I knew they were honking. Geese always honk when they fly. Maybe it's their way of expressing their exhilaration. And yet here I stood, watching them but not hearing them.

As 1988 came to an end, I left corporate America. I was in the first wave of downsized employees. I became a full-time partner with my wife in a business she started the same year I came out of the trees to join corporate America. When I left corporate life, I didn't know if we were going to make it. I didn't know what awaited us at the end of our flight. I *did* know there would be a lot of honking along the way.

My wife and I share a small office in our house. A couple of narrow file cabinets separate our desks. But as small and as cramped as it is, I love this office more than any other I've ever had, because each of our desks faces a window. And I look out any time I choose.

3
Parents' Weekend

A lot more than the seasons changed between my daughter's first and second year away at an upstate New York university.

After getting her settled in a freshman dorm more than a year ago, the drive home was a quiet one. My wife, struggling with the pain of separation, fought back tears. Our son, six years old at the time and still free from the shackles of maturity, didn't bother fighting back his tears. I drove, oblivious to the magnificent scenery of the Adirondacks, focusing on the future. Would she make it? Cut free from the ever-taut guy lines of Mom and Dad, would she successfully navigate the shoals of temptation? Would she exercise the self-discipline required by college studies? Would she party too much? Drink too much? Sleep too little?

I thought back to her junior year in high school when I'd begun the frightening process of letting go. I'd come to see that the bedrock of discipline, so important to her as a child, was gradually becoming a millstone, grinding away at her spirit, stifling her personal growth. And so, I'd told her that I was through punishing. I'd taught her all I could about responsibility. I told her from that time on, the system would punish her for her mistakes.

Now, as I weaved my way back through the ancient mountains, I could only hope she'd understood. The final phase of letting go had begun.

For the next month, I wrote my letters and my wife made her phone calls. There was little sign of homesickness. That was good. Her studies were going well. That was good. She was having a blast. Was that good? I felt like an anxious spectator, holding my breath on the side line of a very important game.

Finally, Parent's Weekend arrived. This was the chance to reassure her. To let her know that mom and dad and younger brother were still real, still within reach. My wife's business kept her from going, but my son and I climbed into my pickup, tuned in the CB, and headed north once again. My daughter had promised her little brother that they'd have a big party and that he could sleep in the dorm with her. He could barely wait.

We arrived on campus, and as we headed for her dorm, I began to feel awkward. For the first time in my life, I'd become a visitor in my daughter's domain. I would have to respect her lifestyle, whatever it was. Suddenly, I realized that I had come as much to reassure myself as to reassure her.

Her greeting was effervescent. Her eyes shone with excitement and enthusiasm. She loved college life, and evidently, it loved her.

I sat down on her bed and, as she and my son discussed the Party Plans, I glanced around the room. A bag of chocolate candy on her desk. Beer bottles on the window sill with cigarette butts floating in opaque liquid. Next to the closet, a half empty bottle of Southern Comfort. I sighed and smiled. And worried.

A bubbling stream of young men and women flowed in and out of the room. Other displaced fathers, hands stuffed in pockets, nodded at me as they passed the open door. Their furtive glances seemed to mirror the same sense of awkward confusion haunting me.

We attended a slide show. A tour of the campus. Then dinner. My daughter's enthusiasm and joy never faltered. The memory of the candy and the booze nagged at me.

After dinner, we returned to the dorm. My son changed into his pajamas and bear-paw slippers. I kissed them good night. Other students drifted in. Rock 'n roll throbbed all around me. I paused in the doorway long enough to see my son dancing on his sister's bed, shouting, "We're gonna paaarty! We're gonna paaarty!"

10

Breakfast the next morning was peppered with yawns and unfocused stares. We drank our last coffee. Said our good-byes. I told her to go back to her dorm and get some sleep, and I hugged her with more love near the surface than I'd felt in years. Finally, my son and I climbed back into the truck and headed home.

She succeeded far beyond my hopes her freshman year. She was home but a month that first summer, choosing instead, to apply for—and win—a position as an orientation leader for incoming freshmen. She became a Keeper of the Rules. A mentor. And with all it's draining demands, she loved it.

After settling her in at the beginning of her sophomore year, the drive home through the mountains was marked, not with tears and silence, but with animated conversation. My wife and I spoke with admiration about our daughter's accomplishments. We talked with enthusiasm about her plans and dreams. Our son chattered excitedly about partying with her again.

When Parent's Weekend arrived the second year, we all piled into my pickup and headed north. My daughter had passed along to us an invitation to a fraternity party. We accepted. This Parent's Weekend was not so much a visit of reassurance as it was a vacation.

We arrived on campus, and as we scuffled through the brilliant autumn leaves to our daughter's dorm, I suddenly realized that a sense of excited anticipation had replaced my awkward apprehension of the year before. I spotted other freshman fathers, their shoulders slightly stooped, their eyes darting, and I said a silent prayer for them and for their sons and daughters.

My daughter's greeting was as effervescent as it had been the year before. She looked slimmer. Her complexion was radiant. Her eyes sparkled.

The room was gorgeous. She and her roommate had set it up so that it looked like a studio apartment. I sat down on her bed, and as she and my wife discussed the decor, I glanced around the room. No candy on her desk. A can of coffee on the window sill. And off in one corner, perched atop a stack of papers and books was a box of 100% whole grain cereal.

A bubbling stream of young men and women drifted in and out of the room. A place for dinner was decided upon. My wife, my daughter and her roommate headed for the door. My son and I followed. I paused at the threshold and glanced back into the room. The floor was clean. The beds were made. Suddenly, I thought of the fraternity party we were going to attend that night. I turned to my son, winked, shook him a little shimmy and crooned, "We're gonna paaarty! We're gonna paaarty!"

4

My Two Fathers

By the time I was 35, I had buried two fathers. One I feared. The other, I loved from a distance.

The one I feared—the one whose genes I carry—was an alcoholic. I don't ever remember feeling close to him even when I was close to him. His life was a war, and whenever I was with him, I was involved in a skirmish.

When I was old enough, he'd take me on his sacred fishing trips. They were tests of endurance for an 8-year-old. Commencing in the raw, hushed pre-dawn hours, they'd unfold on wind-tossed seas, and dissolve in weary, head-nodding rides home.

Pain was the thread running through these rites of passage. I learned how to fish in spite of a sea sick tummy. I learned how to pluck fish hooks from my fingers and grit my teeth against the salt spray that stung the wounds. I learned how to battle sleep when staying awake held more promise than the seduction of fatigue.

I cherish the memories of those pilgrimages, if not the memories of the man who created them, for they taught me that the will is mightier than the flesh.

And yet there are things—deceptively simple things—mightier even than human will. For some like my first father, these things come in bottles. Little by little these things nibble away at human will until nothing remains; nothing but a nightmare of broken promises, foul explosions of irrational rage and long anxiety-filled absences.

I watched this man, my crippled mentor, stagger and fall time and time again until finally, he fell for the last time. At 15, I stood alongside his coffin as I'd so often stood alongside the gunwale of his boat. I stared down at his waxen face and was amazed by his peaceful expression. I felt only relief at his departure. He was in his grave 13 years before I shed my first and final tears for him.

My second father—the one others called my "step" father—was very different from the first. He was a quiet man, humble and self-conscious to a fault.

I was swept up in the maelstrom of adolescence when he came into my life. He seemed disinclined to enter my world and I was too distrustful to invite him in. Still, I was grateful for his love of my mother.

He was a man of labor and brought with him tools I hadn't known existed. He spent his life with us, building and fixing things.

His practical knowledge was encyclopedic, but I was too impatient to read the man well.

When I *did* take the time though, I learned from him. I learned that muscle doesn't get a job done. Persistence gets a job done. Speed loses to patience. "Let the saw do the cutting," he'd say. The older I get, the more I let the saw do the cutting.

But with all he knew, it wasn't enough to make him feel good about himself. He'd turned his back on formal education early in his life, and he considered that an unforgivable blunder. He was often humbled by a flamboyant vocabulary or well-wielded sentence.

Ironically, those whose fancy tool bags contained sheepskins and letters of the alphabet were awed by his artisan's skills. They often sought his advice. He was a fine teacher, clear and direct in his communication. He was always in the homes of others, teaching how this ceiling could be repaired or that cabinet built. These men of letters were more patient than I, and unlike me, had ceilings to repair and cabinets to build. And so they absorbed what would have been my inheritance had I not been romping out of ear shot.

My second father smoked himself to death. One bleak January afternon, I raced to the hospital with him as he braced himself, blanched and tight-lipped, against his third heart attack. I helped seat him in a wheel chair in the emergency room and had no idea it would be the last time he'd stand on his own two feet.

Over the next two weeks, he endured several major operations, including the amputation of his left leg. Finally, he succumbed, but not until I had time to tell him how much I loved him and that he was not the lamb I'd always thought, but a gentle lion.

He faced death with a calmness that shimmed my own faith. "I've been there and back," he said to me a few days before he died. He was referring to his two previous heart attacks. "I'm not afraid." I hoped I'd remember his words when it came *my* turn to stand at The River's edge.

Most men get only one father in life. I got two. From one, I learned courage. From the other, I learned patience. Those are big lessons to teach. Maybe too big for just one man. But I'm doing my best to teach them to my children. Doing my best is all I *can* do. *That* is something I learned from *both* my fathers.

5

A Painful Harvest

We stood to one side of the play ground, a self-conscious covey of parents, sharing, in subdued voices, summer anecdotes. We cast furtive, unappreciated glances at our children as they queued up for a new school year.

Starched dresses, crinkly new blue jeans, scuff-free hightops, spiked hair and stiff, new back packs.

Eyes wide above freckled cheeks and toothless smiles. Shouted greetings. Quick, shy nods of recognition.

Above the fall field of freshly scrubbed faces, the air crackled with hopeful anticipation.

"Maybe I'm crazy," said the mother next to me, "but I'm going to miss my kids being home." Her voice caught on the last word, and she tightened her arms around her stomach.

"Me too." I breathed quickly through my nose to squelch my tears. A mother's September tears are begrudgingly acceptable. A father's, never.

Over the summer, my son and I had become best buddies. It was the first year I'd spent working at home with my wife after being downsized from corporate America. I'd come to share the tapestry of adventures that defined my son's July and August, a privilege denied most fathers.

As week melted into week, we crunched pounds of popcorn in cool, dark theaters, stalked frogs in muddy marshes, played "submarine" and "motorboat" in the town pool, downed dollops of sherbert and ice cream, and stood mesmerized in twilight fields filled with fire flies.

Through the summer, I'd fixed his bike, cleansed his cuts, kissed the hurt out of his bumps, and carried him, countless times, unconscious in his death-like slumber, from our bed to his. In return, he'd given me back my childhood.

"Dad, can we walk into town?

"Dad, let's go down to the bridge. We haven't been there in two whole days.

"Dad, can you take me to MacDonald's?

"When are we going to the movies?

"Can we take the dogs into the fields?

"Are we going to the pool today?"

He ran, skipped, bounced, danced and hopped everywhere. He never walked. Fatigue was intolerable. His or mine. He and his friends scampered in and out of our house enmeshed in their serious dedication to play. Our rooms—now silent—brimmed with the sounds of their shrieks and squeals and squabbling.

There were times when his energy and impatience drove me to the brink of anger. But I was quick to recover, and he was quick to forgive.

Grateful for the best summer I'd had since my own childhood, I kept an eye on the horizon. All too soon, the sun began its gradual slide to the south. The daytime racket of the Cicadas gave way to the evening calls of the Katydids. The air grew chilly, and the crab apples turned a deep red.

One day, the mailman brought papers from school. The bus pass. The room assignment.

I overheard my son and his friends pause in their play to discuss teachers and the burdens of homework.

We went out fishing one last time in the canoe, then I took him shopping for his back pack. Summer was done.

* * *

As the teachers meandered over and introduced themselves to their new charges, I glanced at my wife. She was reading my son's face, and, evidently, was satisfied with what was there.

She'd been through this fall harvest many times before—first with our daughter, now with our son. Her heart had had time to develop calluses. Also, she'd learned over the years to shift her focus to the future. She and my son had already agreed on a back-to-school supper for that evening. And the first of the after-school cup cakes were cooling at that moment on the kitchen counter.

But what was *I* to do? My best buddy was going back to school, and I couldn't go. Aside from work, what would fill my days?

On an impulse, I strolled forward, breaking the unspoken commandment, Thou Shalt Not Embarrass Thy Child in the Presence of Peers.

"See ya, buddy," I said, tapping him lightly on the shoulder. He smiled up at me. "Bye, Dad."

And miracles of miracles, he reached up for a kiss and a hug! I don't know which I felt more - gratitude for this final gesture of love, or pride in his courage to offer it.

As his line marched forward toward the school, he turned and called back, "Can we take the dogs for a run today, Dad?"

I couldn't trust my voice, so I simply gave him a smile and a nod.

6

My College Car

There is a period of about a week every spring when you could tell that American colleges and universities have let out for the summer. You don't have to read about it or know someone attending school. You simply have to walk through your neighborhood and glance at the cars parked curb side.

If any of those cars is: in need of a paint job; sporting a Def Leppard or Grateful Dead sticker (university and college stickers are always found on the *parents'* car); crammed from floor board to ceiling light with laundry, curling irons, dumbbells, bicycles, laundry, milk cartons full of record albums, mismatched and misshapen luggage, laundry, torn posters, stuffed animals, laundry and laundry, then you could safely bet that another college student has alighted for the summer.

Of course, within a week these cars are cleaned out so that they looked like any other cars except for the Grateful Dead stickers and empty beer bottles rolling around on the floor. But they're *not* like any other cars. They're special. They're College Cars.

My College Car was a '62 Chevy station wagon. On the surface, this doesn't sound like the kind of car a college-age youth with turbulent hormones would choose. Below the surface, it was the perfect car for me.

It was as dependable as it was rusty. It had tens of thousands of miles under its fan belt when I bought it, and its once-blue paint job had faded to an exhausted gray. It's shock absorbers were so bad that if I hit a bump in Port Chester, I wouldn't stop bouncing till I reached White Plains. Three of its four doors were sometimes fully operational except in rainy, cold or sunny weather. It sported a genuine, gold-plated coat hanger antennae twisted at the top in the shape of a peace sign. The antennae never got ripped off—even by hawks (you were either a dove or a hawk in those days)—because it looked more like a rug beater that a peace sign.

Since I commuted to school, my College Car was my home-instead-of-home. There was always a pleasant snack aboard, plenty of cold beverage (the kind that would get me in trouble today) and great music pulsing away at the volume I liked best.

Since I was a hunter and fisherman in those days, there was also a seasonally determined sportsman's outfit within easy reach. Fishing poles, tackle boxes and nets in the spring and summer, bow and quiver, shotgun shells, hunting vest and boots in the fall. I spent winters resting up.

For years, I shared my College Car with a close friend—an English setter named Bessie. When the October breeze sparked the blood and the hillsides looked like an impressionist's pallet, Bessie would climb into my College Car and travel to school with me. She'd stretch out in the back, rest her head on my hunting vest, and wait. I'd attend my morning classes, swinging by the car a couple of times between classes to let her out for a quick stretch. After lunch, I'd retrieve my jeans and boots from the car and change in the men's locker room.

I'd point the bow of my College Car north, and a half hour later, Bessie and I would be meandering through woodland and meadow, annoying the daylights out of flight-weary woodcock and life-wary grouse. Bessie and I shared many a sandwich as we gazed contentedly at countless beautiful sunsets through the windshield of my College Car.

Mobility is what made my College Car so special. Whenever I grew restless or bored with the view, I'd simply change it with the turn of a key. I don't remember ever regretting yesterday or worrying about tomorrow when I was riding in my College Car. I only remember changing stations in pursuit of the most satisfying music.

Those days are far behind me now. Bessie and my College Car live only as precious memories. I wonder, as I gaze at this year's crop of College Cars, what special memories their owners are cultivating. It's obvious that some things have changed since my palms cradled the big steering wheel of my Chevy wagon. The cars are shorter today. They sip fuel rather than guzzle it. And their radios sport tape players and quadrophonic speakers.

But one thing, the most important thing, has stayed the same. The highway promises nothing—except possibilities.

7
Birds

One of my greatest joys in life is watching birds. My appreciation of birds dates back to 1950 when I was six years old. That was the year we moved from an apartment building surrounded by concrete and steel to a small house surrounded by bushes and trees.

I remember being captivated by the diversity that characterized the world of birds. The diversity of shapes, sizes, colors, and calls awakened in me a love of nature that had lain dormant beneath the layer of concrete in my first half dozen years of life.

I followed the birds into the fields and woods that surrounded our new home and learned to identify individual species by their songs, their patterns of flight and their plumage.

I collected feathers, treating them like precious little gifts left behind by their owners. To this day, I can't pass by an abandoned primary or tail feather without at least picking it up and examining it. Feathers from several species adorn the sun visor in my pick-up truck, and for whatever reason, I consider them good-luck charms. I'm only a little embarrassed to admit that I believe my truck continues to run well due, in part, to the presence of those feathers.

I do what I can to keep birds in my life. My wife and I share an office in our home. Each of our desks faces a window. I've hung bird feeders in front of each window, and a suet and thistle feeder from a tree branch visible from either window. I've placed a bird bath in the front yard beyond the feeders. I built a platform feeder on our back deck, and I hang a bleeding heart plant outside our kitchen door that's proven itself attractive to hummingbirds.

But it's our feeder in the den window that's most fascinating. It's made of one-way mirrored plastic and shaped like a fish aquarium. I install it each spring by laying it on its side, open end facing out, and bringing the window down to lock it in place—very much like installing a small window air conditioner. I then pour feed onto the floor of feeder. Half of the feeder sticks into the room, and because the walls are one-way mirrors, I can sit inches away from feeding birds without being noticed.

Observing birds often prods me into philosophical musings. For me, birds, along with so many other natural wonders, serve as three-dimensional metaphors for life's most important lessons. Bird watching inspires me to reflect on my own behavior and the behavior of those around me with a more objective eye than I might otherwise use.

For instance, each year there's a small song sparrow that makes his home in our front yard. Our yard faces East, and each morning as the sun inches its way above the horizon, this song sparrow perches on the same oak branch, faces the rising sun and trills a most enchanting melody. I can literally feel my spirit lift within me as I watch and listen to him sing.

Now I'm sure there are ornithologists who would insist he was merely declaring his territorial boundaries or that he was pouring forth his sweet music for some other mundane reason. I don't think so. He always faces the rising sun when he sings, and his posture is open and vulnerable. Personally, I think he's singing out a prayer of gratitude and joy for the gift of another day. If it is a prayer of gratitude, it is also a gift, for it inspires me to utter my own prayer of gratitude, not only for the day, but also for this tiny operatic star and his heavenly instrument.

One of my most thought-provoking bird watching incidents occurred at the mirrored den feeder. I had just finished filling the feeder one afternoon and was in the den when I saw a small finch glide in. He landed belly-deep in food.

Did he start eating? No. Instead, he looked around and seeing several "other" finches, he launched himself into an energetic attack against these interlopers. Of course they were his own reflections. The closer he got to his target, the bigger and more threatening it became. The more fiercely he pecked at it, the more fiercely it pecked back at him. He attacked to the left. He attacked to the right. He attacked the bird in front of him and the one above him. This war went on and on, seeds flying everywhere. I noticed other birds hanging back in nearby trees, all unwilling to expose themselves to possible injury from this one nut case thrashing around in the feeder.

Finally, exhausted and unable to vanquish his attackers despite his most valiant efforts, the finch flew away. Not once during the entire episode did he stop to eat.

That incident made me think about my own life. How often had I stood knee-deep in opportunity only to focus all my attention on imagined threats to my own well-being? How often had I wasted time and energy trying to protect myself against things that didn't exist and banging my head against unyielding walls? How often had others kept their distance from me as I thrashed around, grappling with worries and fears? How often in my life had I "flown away", turning my back on opportunity, too exhausted from my senseless struggle with insecurity to even recognize the opportunity or blessing at my very feet? Probably a lot more often than I was aware.

Observing that little finch has helped my though. Remembering him, I can now hesitate when I find myself in an unfamiliar place. I can hesitate long enough to discern if threats are real or imagined. I can hesitate long enough to invite and allow the input of others I respect. I can hesitate long enough to remember that enjoying good fortune is at least as important as defending it. And above all, I can remember, from observing that little finch, that I will wind up with nothing if I let fear and greed overpower trust and gratitude.

The fact that I can remember all these things doesn't mean I *do* remember all these things. Like most human beings, I need continual reminders. That's why I keep seed in the bird feeders.

27

8
Just a Gull

I was on my walk along the canal one day last spring when I passed two young girls hovering above the body of a dead Black-backed gull. I had come upon the dead gull the day before myself, but it was clear by the pained and confused expression on the faces of the girls - they looked about 10 years old—that they had just made the gruesome discovery.

They looked up at me as I walked by. Feeling compelled to respond to the pain on their faces, the only thing I could think to say was, "Sad, isn't it?"

"Yes!" they both said. Then one asked, "How did it die?"

"Old age and cold nights," I said, surprised by the quickness, choice and certainty of my own response. I kept walking. I didn't want to intrude on their emotions.

I spent the rest of my walk thinking about the dead gull, the pained confusion of the young girls and the question they'd asked me.

Death leaves me feeling confused too. When I'd spotted the gull the day before, I felt sorrow. I wondered if its exit had been acknowledged or honored in some way. We humans have always devised elaborate rituals around death. These rituals seem to help us negotiate the confusing and painful terrain of grief.

Yet, the rest of nature seems to deal with death in a much more matter-of-fact way. It's unusual to come upon the body of a dead animal, especially one that appears to have suffered no injury. Where humans have devised elaborate rituals in response to death, nature has devised elaborate systems of reduction and retrieval. Scavengers of all shapes and sizes lend credence to the phrase "ashes to ashes, dust to dust."

In the natural world, death is simply part of the continuum. Animal remains are quickly and efficiently reduced to original elements and absorbed back into the natural system.

We humans, on the other hand, expend energy and resources to *preserve* the remains of our fellow pilgrims, more or less freezing them in time, deliberately short-circuiting the natural system of decay and absorption. We interrupt the continuum and reflect on the life of the deceased. Individual humans are usually honored at least by reflection if nothing more.

But what about this dead gull? Had it been honored by the other gulls in any way? My immediate response would be "no." But do I know enough about gulls to be sure? Again, "no." They are social, communal beings, that much I do know. They squawk and bicker over perches, fight over food and generally harass one another as they continually violate one another's boundaries.

They do these things in flocks. Together, they soar in dizzying spirals on thermal updrafts above the rippling waves. Together, they hover and dip above schools of feeding bass and bluefish. And together, they hunker down in an irritable silence against the stinging sleet and rain of blasting nor'easters.

So when a member of their community dies, does it go unnoticed? Does it go un-honored? Possibly.

Maybe death is not something to be honored in the world of gulls any more than birth is to be honored. Maybe death is known on some instinctive level to be a natural and predictable juncture in the scheme of things—a setting free of the spirit that inhabited a feathered vessel. A setting free for a far greater flight.

Maybe honoring the dead is part of *our* job, a human obligation just as flying is part of the gull's obligation. Perhaps the two young ladies and I were merely performing an act unique to the human animal. Perhaps death is *supposed* to confuse us—

keep us humble. We are, after all, the only critter equipped not only to *adjust* to a broad spectrum of environments, but also to alter those environments (this has not always worked to our benefit). Perhaps death is a constant reminder that we can create books and buildings and spaceships, but cannot create a seagull. We live life, sometimes destroy life, but we cannot create life. A creative force far greater than ours is required for that.

Whenever we encounter death, we come face to face with our own limitations. Yet, if we reflect on the calm acceptance of death demonstrated by our furred and feathered neighbors, we come to see the continuum. We come to see that we cannot control life, we can simply live it.

Do we live it well? Do we treasure it for the gift it is? These were the questions flitting through my mind as I continued on my walk. Maybe these were the same questions germinating in the minds of the two young girls as they gazed down at the cold, stiff, lifeless body of the gull.

Maybe there is no better way to honor the passing of a life than to have it remind us of our own precious, temporary gift.

9

Going to the Dogs

I read an article in the paper the other morning that made me laugh. It claimed a dog's behavior is determined by the way it's treated in a household rather than by any characteristics attributed to its breed. I read parts of the article out loud to my four companions—the four dogs with whom we share our home. They were unimpressed.

Each morning, the dogs and I start our day the same way. We climb into our mini-van, drive to the coffee shop for my wife's papers, a cup of coffee, a fat-free muffin, and then we head down to Cape Cod canal. There, parked at the mouth of Cape Cod bay, I have my breakfast, sharing the muffin with all four dogs. (I don't know why I haven't lost weight.) If I leave the dogs home, there's hell to pay. Believe me, it's easier to risk being labelled Cape Cod's Jed Clampett than it is to leave those dogs home.

I'll introduce them in order of age, oldest to youngest. First is Holly. She's 16 and in excellent health. She's a mixed breed—my wife was duped into buying her one Christmas for $20 from a pet shop owner who swore she was a Pekingese. Pick-a-nose is more like it. Holly looks like a cross between a Shelty and a miniature Golden retriever. She's a calm dog, exceptionally intelligent, and, when it serves her needs, she's partially deaf.

Ginger is next. A small, gray Yorkshire terrier, approximately 10 years old, she was rescued by my wife from a different, and I should add indifferent pet shop owner. Ginger had become unpopular and unwanted in the shop owner's household after the arrival of twins. Ginger came to us frightened and depressed, her fine hair dirty and knotted with her own feces.

Next is Mookie, a six-year-old miniature, black Yorkshire terrier. The only male, he is our daughter's dog and lived with her until her recent move to an apartment that won't allow pets. Not four-legged ones anyway. They had no objection to her corn snake. Mookie is nuts. Just plain nuts. I'll get into that later.

Last, but very far from least, is Lucy. A two-year-old, black mini-Dachshund, she's a ten pound dog with a 300 pound attitude. Lucy is convinced my wife is her mother and sticks to her like gum to the bottom of a sneaker.

All four dogs eat the same food from the same dish, drink the same water from the same bowl, go out attended but unleashed at the same time to relieve themselves on our same half acre of woods and come back in at the same time to resume their same day-long naps. Yet, each of them is as different from the other as a chicken is from a penguin.

Holly is quiet, observant and is always either sleeping or thinking. I swear she understands English. She knows exactly what we say and what our intentions are throughout the day. She's tolerant and easy going. She's self-controlled except when it comes to two things; my neighbor's compost pile and grapes.

The grapes are no problem. Whenever I'm snacking on grapes, she sits in front of me with an expression on her face that borders on hysteria. The desperation in her expression slowly melts away as I share my grapes with her. Sometimes the other dogs insist on having a grape too, just to make sure they're not missing out on something good, but they always lose interest quickly and cast Holly sideway glances of disgust as they amble back to their napping positions.

My neighbor's compost pile is another story. He's continually adding kitchen scraps to the pile. Occasionally, Holly gets sidetracked by the odoriferous pile, particularly during her night time toilet obligations. Her hearing mysteriously lapses, and as I thrash around looking for her, my blood pressure escalating, she angles her way through the undergrowth to consummate her rendezvous with the compost pile. Whenever I discover her there, she skulks back toward the house feigning guilt and remorse.

But the worst is yet to come. Unlike the grapes, her snacking at the compost pile raises havoc with her digestive tract, rendering it volcanic. Over the years we've become quite knowledgeable about rug and fabric cleaners, and Holly has spent a number of lonely nights in the basement, erupting.

Ginger, the ignored Yorky, has regained her self-confidence in the years she's lived with us. In fact, she's gone to the other extreme and has become our self-appointed head of security. She barks at everyone and everything. She barks at the mailman everyday. She barks at the UPS driver, the neighbors, the neighbors' kids, the neighbors' dogs, my son's friends, my son, my wife, our two cats, me and the T.V. set whenever a doorbell rings in some sit-com. In the car, she barks at the guy pumping gas, the patrons entering and exiting the coffee shop, the people strolling along the canal and even the sea gulls at the canal. She get particularly annoyed and vocally abusive if I dare share a few crumbs of our morning muffin with the birds at the canal.

Ginger's barking always sets off the other dogs. I think they feel obligated out of a sense of guilt for sleeping all day to defend the hearth, and so they race from room to room or from front seat to back seat bumping into one another, barking their fool heads off with no one but Ginger knowing why they're barking.

If one of us is on the phone when Ginger incites one of her chaotic uprisings, we frequently lose our own self-control and add to the insanity by bellowing for them to shut up. More often than not they interpret this as encouragement, and the melee reaches new heights. By the time things wind down and Holly stops barking (Holly's own barking makes her hearing even worse, and she can't tell when the others have stopped, so she just carries on), Ginger is curled up somewhere where it's quiet, resting up for her next false alarm.

Next is Mookie. As I said earlier, Mookie is nuts. When he

came to live with us, my daughter claimed his behavior had really begun to deteriorate. She claimed he'd begun to act downright mean. He'd snapped at her a few times and even attacked visitors. When she moved, we volunteered to take him. Sending Mookie to us was kind of like sending him to a rehab.

He was fine for about three days. Suddenly, one night, he jumped up from a sound sleep, scurried behind our couch, and started growling and barking. When we headed upstairs to bed that night, he raced up ahead of us, scooted under our bed and continued the bazaar, aggressive behavior for a couple of hours. Finally, he went to sleep, only to wake several hours later and begin this nonsense again.

This behavior went on for days. My wife and I grew groggy and irritable from lack of sleep. As I observed his behavior night after night, I began to notice certain characteristics. First, the unusual behavior would commence only after the sun set and it got dark outside. Second, each incident would start with him whipping around, checking his behind, growling, then flying for cover. Third, he became oblivious to any words of encouragement or reassurance. In fact, he'd growl, snarl and rage at anyone who tried to calm him.

Our local vet had no idea what caused the radical behavior. I was at a loss, until I finally figured it out. Watching him whip around one night at the onset of one of his episodes, I suddenly understood.

Mookie is haunted. He has butt ghosts. I've never seen them, but I have seen Mookie see them, and it's not a pretty sight. These malicious, invisible creatures emerge after dark, grab Mookie by the butt and set him off. Once they grab him, trust goes out the window, and Mookie is swept up in a maelstrom of terror. Behind the couch he goes where he need defend himself on only two fronts rather than four.

Why Mookie is the only one of our dogs susceptible to butt ghosts is beyond me. It would take a specialist trained in both dog psychology and parapsychology to answer that question. Perhaps it's the same reason some humans are more psychic than others. Or perhaps it's genetic. Maybe Mookie is deficient in the gene that stimulates the production of butt-ghost anti-toxin (BGAT). Whatever the reason, Mookie's life became a living hell when the sun went down.

I was at a complete loss on how to help him until I stumbled upon the solution one night by mistake.

Whenever he was under attack by the butt ghosts, he refused to join the other dogs for his night time walk. Instead, he'd hunker down behind the couch and defend himself against incoming marauders.

I couldn't have him using the house as a bathroom, so before the sun set one night, I clipped a long leash on him. This way, when I was ready to take the other dogs for their walk, I could pull him out from under the couch and drag him along with us.

It worked like a charm. When it was time, I pulled the cord and out came Mookie. But that's not all that happened. For some unknown reason, the butt ghosts ceased their attack on him and went into full retreat.

I'm not sure why the leash makes a difference, but it does. Perhaps the leash attaches Mookie more strongly to my dimension than to the dimension of the butt ghosts. Perhaps my own BGAT hormone travels from me through the leash to Mookie like electricity through a wire, thereby immunizing him against the assault of the butt ghosts. Whatever the reason, Mookie behaves almost normally when he's wearing the leash. And for Mookie, any behavior even hinting at normality is nothing short of miraculous.

I have no doubt the butt ghosts are still around, constantly patrolling the borders of Mookie's reality, looking for a weak spot, a point of entry. But as long as we keep the leash handy, the little guy is safe.

And finally, there's Lucy. Our mini-dachshund, has been with us for the shortest time. Yet, I have never seen *any* critter, let alone such a small dog, rearrange an entire household to meet its own needs as thoroughly, as quickly and as efficiently as Lucy has rearranged us.

She started from day one by refusing to stay in her bed in

the kitchen at night. She overcame every barrier I designed and built, struggling with all the strength in her tiny body to ascend the stairs leading to our bedroom. Night after night, we'd wake to her whining and howling at the foot of our bed.

Exhaustion wore down our resistance and forced our surrender. One night, my wife reached down, scooped her up and dropped her on the bed between us. Lucy wormed her way under the covers, burrowed down to our feet, scratched together an imaginary nest, curled up and fell sound asleep. She's been there ever since.

When she decides it's time for us to wake up, she travels like a mole from our feet to our faces and starts licking and poking us until it's less annoying to get up than it is to stay in bed.

Lucy is Ginger's second-in-command regarding home security. Lucy barks louder and with more ferocity than the other dogs. She bullies anything and anyone that exhibits the slightest fear of her, particularly if there's a pane of glass or screen door separating her from her target. Her bravery is inversely proportional to the distance between her and her attackee.

This false bravado backfired on her one day. A large slow-witted mutt showed up at our front screen door. Lucy bolted out from her hiding place under the ottoman and began subjecting this simple oaf to one of her more arrogant tongue lashings. The screen door was hooked at the top, and Lucy knew it. She was throwing herself against the bottom of the door with confident enthusiasm when, without warning, the bottom part of the door opened. She tumbled out, and the door snapped shut behind her.

She turned and looked at the door with an expression of total disbelief. Then she turned and gazed up at the big lummox she'd been challenging to a life and death fight only seconds before. Instantly, he became a long lost friend. She scampered around him, whining and wagging her tail in the most shameless display of hypocritical submissiveness I've ever witnessed. I was so embarrassed, I had to turn away.

Luckily, the big guy mistook her antics as a genuine display of friendship, and he didn't swallow her. She continued her phony display until I let her back in the house, at which point she resumed her belligerent insults.

Perplexed, the big guy looked up at me, yawned, then loped away. Lucy barked at him until he was out of sight. Then she gave me a disgusted look and headed back under the ottoman. I do notice, though, that she never jumps against the screen door anymore.

So there it is. Four dogs living in the same household, each very different from the other: Holly, the consummate con-artist, Ginger the security-minded worry wart, Mookie the psychically challenged schizophrenic, and Lucy the loveable little tyrant.

All I can say is that it's a good thing *I'm* normal!

10
Home

In 1969, I bought the first house I ever owned. It has no attic, no basement, and no garage. I didn't carry a mortgage, choosing instead to pay cash in full. Sixty five dollars. Plus tax.

It's a 10 by 10 umbrella tent—a canvas home—and the equity it's built over the decades has enriched my spirit rather than my bank account.

The scenes I've gazed at through its front door more than make up for its dearth of closet space. The fragrances that have drifted in through its walls and back window more than compensate for the fact that the cook must brave the elements while in the kitchen. And the occasional long walks in the dark to the bathroom are a small price to pay for the sweet evening orchestrations of crickets, frogs and katydids that so often lull me to sleep.

My canvas home rests atop the foundation of so many lovely memories. Like the long weekend I anchored its corners in the sand of an endless beach in northern California. Each night I would lie back on my air mattress, close my eyes, and drift to sleep, rocking on the rhythmic primal pounding of the surf.

One night, while camped at the edge of a pond in New Hampshire, I was startled awake by a family of beavers slapping their tails against the still surface of a nearby pond.

I recall a camp site in central Florida where the air was laced with the heady perfume of the blossoms on the orange trees surrounding my canvas home.

And I remember camp sites in the Wyoming forests where

the floor of my canvas home was cushioned on beds of pine needles. The memory of that melancholy fragrance can calm my agitated spirit to this day.

Like all homes, my canvas home bears the scars inflicted by time. I've replaced corner shock cords snapped by a wind storm on the Finger Lakes of New York. I've sewn the window, rent by a falling limb in central Jersey. And I've patched a hole discovered in the floor during a hurricane on Cape Cod.

But like any home of quality and substance, and like any home cared for with love, my canvas home survives. And it continues to feed not only my spirit, but the spirits of my wife and children as well.

This summer, we were camped on a river bank in Pennsylvania. Across the river, there was a fallow field—part of an Amish farm left alone for the year to recharge itself. The field was overgrown with weeds and wild flowers.

Each night we were treated to one of the most spectacular sights we've ever seen in nature. Tens of thousands of fireflies would rise up out of the weeds and tangles of that field into the darkness above. It was as if the earth were releasing thousands upon thousands of wavering golden threads. That silent display has become one of the most tranquil and serene memories of my life.

Not long ago, I was meandering through a sporting goods store. I spotted the latest model of my canvas home set up in a far corner of the store. I walked over and glanced at the price tag. I let out a low whistle when I saw the amount. Nearly five times what I'd paid 25 years ago. If I were to purchase it today, I'd have to mortgage it with my credit card.

Then I considered the treasure chest of memories that no person or circumstance would ever be able to take from me, and I walked away, knowing some things are worth the investment no matter what the cost.

11
Labor of Love

Like most adult males, it takes a lot to make me cry. But there I was, rolling west on Cape Cod's mid-cape highway with tears spilling down my cheeks.

It was Labor day. My wife and I were heading back to our new home in Sandwich after returning the rental truck we'd used to transport our family and belongings from our home in New York. We were physically and emotionally exhausted, not only from moving, but also from maintaining as best we could, our hectic business schedule.

As we drove along, we saw crowds of people lining the overpasses, waving to us. They held banners and signs wishing us well, and we suddenly realized they were saying good-bye to all the tourists leaving the Cape. These were the bridge parties we'd heard about.

Flabbergasted and overwhelmed by the magnanimous gesture, we each began to cry. The strain of our journey and memories of all we'd endured in the recent months were still fresh within us. It was almost too much to believe the journey was done, that we were headed back to our own home, and that we were settling into a community where people cared enough to wish well to strangers in such a real and vivid way.

We hurried home, tore off a piece of cardboard from the mountain of unpacked boxes in our living room, wrote a message in oversized letters, and raced back to the overpass nearest us. We joined the small crowd waving at the river of traffic flowing beneath the bridge.

While we were waving and alternating arms to relieve tired muscles, a car pulled up alongside the curb behind us. A young man helped an old lady out of the passenger's side. She limped painfully to the edge of the bridge and joined all of us waving good-bye. As I watched her, I could tell she'd done this before. Perhaps many times. I could see, to her, and to the others on the bridge, this was an annual tradition.

Suddenly, I felt a melancholy connection with the tourists leaving as well as with the people on the bridge. I knew the stream of travelers well; their stomachs tense; attention focused on the road before them; eyes flicking over gauges and mirrors; destination somewhere out in front. I knew the people on the bridge too; settled; peaceful; waving farewell to the migratory ones; breathing sighs of relief as the frenetic energy of summer melted away in the quiet autumn dusk.

I felt connected and disconnected at the same time. I considered the stone bridge I was standing on and realized I was on an emotional bridge as well. For nearly 20 years, my wife, my children and I had lived in houses owned by others. We'd been travelers, striving for a destination, never really connected to our communities, never really connected to a home we could call our own.

Now, all that had changed. Our home belonged to us, and we belonged to our community. We were no longer travelers. We'd reached our destination.

I smiled at the enthusiastic reactions from those whizzing beneath us. Some leaned out of their cars and waved back. Others shouted and whistled. Some, I could see, were crying as I had been earlier.

While we waved, we spoke with our neighbors on the bridge. They were amused to hear we'd only arrived the previous day, yet we were there with them on the bridge. I explained that in our old home, a crowd gathered on an overpass was sometimes there to throw down things other than blessings on the travelers below. What better way to begin our new life here on Cape Cod than to take part in such a humane and decent tradition as a bridge party?

44

One young woman leaned over and asked, "What does your sign say?"I turned the sign toward her. "SAFE HOME! . . ." she read out loud. "I like that. That's nice."

She had no way of knowing just *how* nice.

12
Stick and Speedo

Though I've been married for more than 20 years, I understand next to nothing about the relationship between men and women. I'm not being humble here. I'm being honest.

Having said that, I'll now crawl a little farther out on the limb and describe one of the differences between men and women that I've noticed recently. I call this particular difference the Stick and Speedo phenomenon. It's a variation of the universal natural law, Opposites Attract. I've labeled this the Stick and Speedo phenomenon based on an incident that occurred between my wife and me a couple of years ago. But let me digress briefly.

I tend to move slowly. It's my style. I don't like to rush anywhere. Rushing agitates me. Rushing makes me irritable.

I like to mosey. As I move forward through time, I like to observe what's going on all around me, not just what's going on in front of me. Moseying affords me this luxury of observation. When I mosey, I feel content. Serene. At peace with the world. Sometimes, I run into other people who also like to mosey. Occasionally, I'll find myself in long conversations with these people, exchanging stories about our lives, sharing feelings that you might share with old friends. Often, when we go our separate ways, I feel as though I've made a new friend. It's all part of the moseying experience.

My wife does not like to mosey. The verb itself, let alone the act, agitates her. She's a Point A to Point B person. The only observation she wants to make is that Point B is looming larger, quicker.

Most of the time, this difference between us doesn't cause problems. I do my things my way. She does her things her way.

Every once in awhile, however, our diverse styles clash. Usually this happens when we go shopping together.

Now to the incident resulting in the Stick and Speedo label. A couple of years ago, my wife and I were in a mall together. I was walking in front of her. Finally, she stepped briskly around me and assumed the lead. She tried to get me to walk faster by encouraging me with, "Move over, Speedo! I've never seen anyone walk so slowly. How do you do it? If I walked that slow, I'd fall over. One foot would be in the air too long, I'd lose my balance, and over I'd go. What you need is a stick up your butt!"

I smiled at her, and as she faded somewhere into my future, I called out, "I married *you*, didn't I?"

From that day forward, we each wore our nicknames with pride. She's "Stick". I'm "Speedo". At Christmas, she even gave me a gold key ring shaped like a heart with the inscription, "To Speedo, from Stick."

Whenever this incident comes up in discussions, other couples inevitably have their own Stick and Speedo stories to relate. What's interesting, however, is that the phenomenon does not seem to be gender-specific. In some cases the men were Sticks and the women were Speedos. In some cases, vice versa.

Now, according to Carl Jung, the famed analyst, both men and women possess an animus and an anima, giving rise to both masculine and feminine character traits. So too does it appear that each sex possesses both Stick and Speedo traits, though one set of traits does appear dominant depending on the individual.

For instance, even though I'm predominantly a Speedo, I definitely possess Stick traits that bubble to the surface when I drive. If I find myself driving behind someone who is moseying —let's say 10 miles *under* the speed limit—I try to encourage them to move a little faster. This encouragement may take the form of animated, less-than-complimentary, verbal dialogue, which of course the other driver can't hear. If the circumstance remains unchanged for an extended period, I may transcend my Speedo personality entirely and for a brief period become a full-blown Stick. I then compliment my one-sided dialogue with animated physical gesticulations. Whenever I experience this temporary metamorphosis, I feel both exhilarated and exhausted. I'm always happy to return to the land of Speedo, but I must acknowledge a certain thrill in having visited the land of Stick.

I've noticed that my wife occasionally displays her recessive Speedo character traits, particularly when dealing with people on the phone. Once I heard her talking to someone, going on at great length about how her day had progressed. Uninterrupted, she spoke quietly about her most recent aches and pains, about how one of our dogs had been sprayed by a skunk just before bolting into the house and throwing up on the rug, how our finances were a shambles, and how upset she was that particular day with the national and international news.

The conversation seemed to end abruptly. When she moseyed into the kitchen where I was, I asked her, "Who was that, your mom?"

"No," she said, a complacent smile spreading across her face. "It was one of those telephone sales guys. He asked me how I was doing today, so I told him. He hung up while I was analyzing the recent change in weather. Imagine that, Speedo, he hung up on me."

I shook my head. "Hard to imagine, Stick, someone being that rude."

13

The Sandal Family

Logic and efficiency are the most desirable characteristics in problem solving. Who would disagree with that statement? Not I. Recently, though, I learned that using logic and efficiency is *not* always the best way to solve a problem.

Close to our home there's a quarter-mile-long boardwalk. The boardwalk spans a sprawling tidal marsh and the creek that snakes in from the sea that feeds the marsh. After crossing the creek and marsh, the boardwalk rises up the slope of a sand dune and comes to an end at the top of the dune. Standing at the end of the boardwalk, visitors are afforded a breathtaking view of Cape Cod Bay.

The boardwalk attracts tourists and residents alike. When I tend to my daily chores—banking, post office, supermarket, etc., I often head down to the boardwalk with a coffee and a pair of binoculars.

I was on one of these breaks when I learned a lesson about problem solving.

It was a brilliant summer day—blue sky, puffy white clouds, balmy breeze—and I was moseying along the boardwalk, heading for the beach at the far end when I encountered a young family returning along the walk. There was a mom, a dad and several young children, the youngest appearing to be about three years old. Just as we passed one another, the youngest tripped. His sandal slipped off and sailed over the edge of the boardwalk. It landed with a thump in the black mud exposed by the dropping tide. The youngster got very upset, and a pleasant outing quickly deteriorated into a minor crisis.

The sandal lay on the mud about four feet below the boardwalk. I hesitated, then walked back to them to see if I could help retrieve the sandal and avert the crisis.

I analyzed the problem and came up with an easy, efficient solution. One of us would lie down on our back on the boardwalk, hold the youngest child by the ankles, lower him, upside down to the sandal, then lift him up to the boardwalk again. No problem.

I was just about to impose my solution on them and calm the growing confusion when I heard a shout. We all turned in time to see dad leap off the boardwalk 15 feet away and land with a loud "thlump!" in the tidal mud.

He sunk to his knees and began struggling to extricate himself. All of us stared in shock, and when he looked up to find us staring at him, he laughed.

His laugh changed everything. His wife started laughing. His kids started laughing, including the little one, who only moments before had been wailing in frustration, and of course, I started laughing.

Suddenly, dad had an audience, and he transformed himself into a wonderful actor.

He worked each leg free of the goop, then thumped it down again, looking like a drunken sumo wrestler. He growled and howled as mud spurted up around him, spattering his clothes, face and hair. He swung his arms in front of himself. One moment he was a frustrated gorilla, the next a timid monster. Other people on the boardwalk stopped to watch and join in the laughter.

He howled at the sky, slogging through the muck, all the time working closer and closer to the sandal

At this point, the members of his family were doubled over with hysterics. The youngest was laughing so hard that I think he may have wet his pants.

"I'm the creature from the Black Lagooooon!! . . .," dad crowed as he arrived directly below us. He reached down, snatched up the sandal and tossed it up onto the boardwalk. Then he boosted himself up and flopped onto the boardwalk like a muddy seal.

Still laughing, I turned and headed out toward the beach. The sandal family worked their way back toward the parking lot at the beginning of the boardwalk. I could hear their laughter and chatter like bird song recede as the distance between us grew.

By the time I reached the foot of the sand dune, the sandal family had reached the parking lot. Though I could no longer hear them, I saw dad wade knee-deep into the creek and wash himself clean of the mud.

At the end of the boardwalk there's a bench to sit on. It's perched right at the top of the dune. I sat on the bench, gazing out over the bay and thought about what I'd just been through.

I knew my solution for retrieving the sandal had been the quickest and most efficient. However, I now understood that it would not have been the most desirable. Spontaneity and whimsy had provided the best, albeit sloppiest, solution.

Not only had the sandal been retrieved, but the family had been left with one of the most wonderful memories of their lives. The youngest would not recollect his anger, shame and frustration over losing the sandal, but he would never forget the sight of his mud-spattered dad howling gleefully at the summer sky. Dad had humbled himself enough to be laughed at... and loved more.

The lost sandal, starting out as a source of frustration and potential anger, had ended up being a catalyst for joy.

And I had come to recognize that logic and efficiency are not always the best way to solve a problem. Sometimes these two qualities must take a back seat to spontaneity and humor.

It was the humor I thought about the most. How often do we incorporate humor in problem solving? Almost never. We become far too concerned with the speed of our solutions, far too busy with either attacking the source of the problem, be it a person or a circumstance, or too busy defending ourselves if we contributed to the problem.

What a wonderful opportunity humor offers us. It dissolves blame, eliminates the need for self-defense and sometimes reduces the problem itself to almost inconsequential proportions. At least it had done so in the sandal family incident. No one had been left with hurt feelings, and everyone had been left with a wonderful memory. And the mud had washed off with a little salt water.

14
Change

Often, I'm acutely aware of how fast the world around me is changing. It's reached the point (or maybe it's always been the point) that the only constant *is* change. I'm far less aware of how much I've changed over the years. Usually, a specific event will startle me into facing how much I've changed while being completely unaware that the change was taking place. Such an event occurred last Christmas.

My daughter—now in her mid-20's—was home for the holidays. It was Christmas morning. She and my teenage son were sitting on the floor in front of the tree unwrapping presents. The sound of Christmas carols was drifting in from the stereo in the den. My wife was just finishing up the first batch of breakfast waffles, and I was sitting back sipping a cup of hot coffee, saying a silent prayer of thanks for all the blessings in my life.

At one point my daughter stood up and walked over to me. She extended one leg, turning it sideways so I could see her ankle. "Look, Dad. I got a tattoo. Do you like it?"

I stared down at her foot and there, in bold, bright colors, was a happy little fish, blowing a stream of bubbles up toward her calf. Suddenly, my son appeared behind her, extending his hand toward me. He was holding a small white box. "Look at this cool new earring I got, Dad!"

I admired each of their latest acquisitions, let each of them know, and it wasn't until they'd returned to their places in front of the tree that I became aware of what had just happened.

My daughter had shown me her new tattoo, my son had shown me his newest earring, and I hadn't found the episode unusual in any way.

Had you told me, when I was my daughter's age, that someday I'd have a tattooed daughter and a son who wore earrings and that they would be normal and admirable in every way, I would have helped you find a bed in a mental institution. Yet here it was, which makes me wonder how many people are shuffling around in mental institutions, heavily sedated for merely being prophetic.

The thing that fascinated me was not my daughter's tattoo or my son's earring but rather my simple acceptance.

When I was growing up in the 50's, behavior of the sexes was clearly and rigidly defined. There were no males wearing earrings. If there had been, they would have been targets for abusive behavior. The only place tattooed women could be found was in the circus.

Then along came the 60's. American conventions and authority were not only questioned, they were challenged, and in a rash of ugly events, assassinated. The day John Kennedy was murdered, more than a man died.

God knows, we needed change. The rigidity of our beliefs and behavior was steering us toward nuclear annihilation. Women and people of color in our nation were suffering abuse, and we still believed that children should be seen and not heard. We even deluded ourselves into believing that our young were old enough to die in rice paddies halfway around the world, but that they were not responsible enough to put one or another sleazy politician in office.

It seems incomprehensible to me that we clung to those values with such fierce inflexibility. But cling we did, and so forces of change hit us all the harder. Elvis, The Beatles, The Rolling Stones ignited us and we set aflame our draft cards, our bras, and our cities. The Pill gave everyone some heavy breathing room. We reached for the stars and landed, feet first, on the moon. We lost a war and gained a conscience. And two young men named Steve, hunched over a pile of electronic ganglia were about to create the Apple of our eye and launch a computer revolution that would help ensure change as a way of life.

Though we've been evolving incessantly as a species, I believe the two decades between 1950 and 1970 were one of the most accelerated periods of change in recent history. Change was occurring so rapidly in this country during the later part of the Nixon administration that I feared authority was going to try and force it to slow down by declaring Marshall law, or worse yet our entire nation was going to stumble into a second civil war.

Fortunately, neither tragedy happened. The Age of Aquarius was ushered in and opposing forces settled into a grudging acceptance of one another.

Though it's sometimes hard for me to accept, I do believe this environment of change is both necessary and desirable. Evolution demands change.

If I used the daily news as a yardstick of evolution, I'd be tempted to say that we're evolving backwards. However, for some reason, good news doesn't hold our attention (it lacks the shocking power of bad news), so what we really see and hear each day is the bad news or the upsetting news. We're like that fellow Mark Twain once quoted: "I'm an old man who has known many troubles, most of which never happened."

I'm not naive. I know that there are a lot of troubles in life. As this is being written, there are approximately three dozen armed conflicts going on around the world. But I also know from half a century of personal experience, that the vast majority of people are decent, ethical, moral and weary. Adjusting and readjusting to change, meeting life's daily demands, and steering clear of life's bozos makes all of us weary. But with rare exception, these demands and expectations have not destroyed our sense of responsibility to our families, our communities and our fellow humans.

It's the unusual that makes the news, and that only serves to call attention to it. When these travesties are exposed in the heat of the spotlight, the violators are often forced to change; to evolve in a more humane direction. Not always, but often. As our world grows smaller through the immediacy of communication, we become more tolerant of one another and less tolerant of aberrant, destructive behavior, which, decades and centuries ago we weren't even aware of. Because of change, many of the despots and maniacs among us can no longer escape our attention. We may feel frustrated right now by our uncertainty in how to deal with them, but at least they no longer escape our attention.

The way I see it, change has improved my life. It has forced me to remain flexible, and this flexibility has led me to greater tolerance. More tolerance has led me to more opportunity.

So when my daughter shows me her tattoo or my son shows me his latest earring, I'm not going to judge them or berate them or punish them because of some rigid belief that I was expected to hold onto for decades. Instead, I choose to see my children as individuals growing up in a world of change. If they are to function well in this world, they must feel comfortable with change, not threatened by it.

I've come to see that the most valuable gift I can give my children, next to love, is acceptance. I didn't always know this, but I know it now. I don't always practice it well, but I try. I'm changing.

15
Our Street

It's twilight, and I'm sitting on our front steps, staring at his house. Like each house on our street, it's small and modest. Red shakes. White trim. Square lawn, rich green, corner to corner to corner. He'd had the roof done last year.

As I sit in the failing light, I glance at the other houses on our street. Like each of us who live in them, the houses are similar in the image they present to the outside world. And like each of us, they're very much different inside.

The birds are squabbling now over their evening roosts. Far away, I hear a train's whistle as it passes through a station.

It's hot, and the windows are open in the houses on our street. Snatches of conversation drift out into the evening. Here and there, televisions defy the night with their frenetic dance of blue-gray light.

I squint and tilt my head, struggling to comprehend what exactly it is that has happened to us. Suddenly, I see the houses on our street as I've never seen them before. I see them as containers. Two-story containers overflowing with the stuff of our daily lives; shoes and socks, pots and pans, hammers and nails. Two-story containers, cradling our memories; letters, photos, cards and trophies. Two-story containers sustaining our dreams; hope chests and catalogues, blueprints and bank accounts.

Yet they are more, these houses on our street. They're pinpoints of our existence. Howie and Sue live over here. Bob and Polly up there. Ted and Pat over there. We're always in the present tense, even when we're out. And on some deeper level, we're connected, those of us on our street. Connected, just as our houses are connected by cracked and weather-worn sidewalks. When one of us hurts, on some deeper level, we all hurt.

My wife saw him Saturday. A wet spot beneath his van had stopped him short, she told me. He'd popped the hood, checked things out, then apparently satisfied all was well, he'd closed the hood and backed the van into his driveway.

He always backed in, setting himself up for the next day. But his van didn't move the next day. Nor the next. At night, there were no lights. No sounds. The neighbors on each side of him grew uneasy. They dialed his number and listened as the phone rang and rang and rang.

Finally, the neighbor on his right—the one to whom he'd entrusted his key for emergencies when he was away—went in. The neighbor found him on the couch where he'd lain down two days before to rest.

No violence. No struggle. Just a quiet passing into the arms of the Dark Angel.

* * *

It's night now. The mosquitoes are becoming hard to ignore, but I sit anyway. I can't bring myself to get up and turn my back on his house.

It's still full of his stuff, and yet it's empty. His van waits, facing the street. The irony of its license plate strikes me: LETS-GO2.

We are quiet this week, those of us on our street. One of us is gone, and all of us are wounded. When we see each other, we pause and huddle and stare at our feet. We speak hesitantly, in subdued voices about our vulnerability and our misplaced priorities. And we see, through our hurt and confusion, that we are family.

He would have liked that.

16
Washashores

The first time I heard the term "washashore" was at a wildlife lecture. A local biologist was delivering the lecture at our library about one of Cape Cod's least understood residents, the coyote. I was seated next to a loquacious, elderly woman with a mischievous twinkle in her eye.

"Where are you from?" she asked as we settled in, waiting for the lecture to begin.

"We moved here from New York," I said.

"Oh!" she said with a laugh, "You're washashores!"

It took a moment for me to grasp the meaning and the implication of the term. When I did, I laughed with her. "Yes. I guess that's just what we are—washashores."

The term brought back memories. I grew up in Rye, New York, a suburb of New York City bordered on its eastern edge by Long Island Sound. In my youth, I loved walking along the shoreline, scanning the receding tidal line for interesting curiosities that had been relinquished by the sea. These were the washashores - fragments of people's lives or mysterious natural wonders that teased my imagination.

As time passed and congestion grew on the periphery of Long Island Sound, the washashores changed. Plastic, styrofoam and other seedy garbage washed up on the beaches along with the good stuff. Fecal counts rose. Used prophylactics and syringes gave beach walkers the shivers.

So, when this lady referred to us, tongue-in-cheek, as

washashores, the images in my mind were vivid to say the least.

"Who is *not* considered a washashore?" I asked.

"Only direct descendants of the pilgrims," she said.

Just as I suspected. The term 'washashore' was derisive in origin.

"Are you a descendant of the pilgrims?"

"No," she said, smiling again. "I'm a second generation washashore."

Of course, the irony is that the pilgrims were really Cape Cod's first washashores. They literally washed ashore in what is now Provincetown, then sailed across Cape Cod Bay to what eventually became Plymouth.

I'm quite sure the pilgrims were more concerned with surviving their first winter here than they were about their social status. If any group had a right to indulge in self-importance, it would have been the native Americans who taught the pilgrims the skills that got them through those first harsh winters.

I suspect several generations had to come and go before the descendants of these original washashores had time and resources to construct a social hierarchy.

I don't know why we humans do this to one another - place ourselves and others on the rungs of a ladder of importance and worth. Perhaps it's an outgrowth of nature's pecking order, a hierarchy based on strength and aggression.

If it is an outgrowth of nature's pecking order, it's certainly an aberrant one. Physical strength and aggression have become irrelevant. In fact, exercising those two qualities can actually jeopardize the solid footing of someone standing on a high rung of our social ladder.

Economics has become the engine driving our contemporary hierarchy. Money leads to education, leads to opportunity, leads to status, leads to influence, leads to money, leads to education . . . etc.

Of course not everyone with lots of money and/or opportunity chooses to enter this loop, but it's definitely a closed circle to those without the gilt. In past millennia, our ancestors of power *carried* the right club. Today, they *belong* to the right one.

62

Perhaps social hierarchy is an outgrowth of the human need for love, admiration and respect. This emotional currency validates us and reinforces our worth. Since we exist on a plane of relativity—good needs bad, up needs down, right needs left to define themselves by the relative contrast of their opposites—maybe social hierarchy emerged relative to our need for approval. Those seeking approval most fiercely must brand others with disapproval. Since we're all fundamentally the same beneath our epidermis, the characteristics differentiating us and placing us on one rung or another must be external. So, our cars, our clothes, our homes, our educations, our vocabularies become more than functional tools. They become components of a label. These labels then either raise or lower our status. Or so we believe.

Actually, it's a lot of nonsense. That's why the woman in the library couldn't help but smile when she labelled me (and herself) washashores.

Thank goodness most people recognize that the concept of social hierarchy falls apart when one looks back far enough over time. The truth is that we're *all* washashores. Not just humans, but *all* land dwellers. We're all progeny of the sea.

A billion or so years ago the ancestors of all land dwellers crawled out of the prehistoric soup and established the first colonies on land. Those organisms were the first true pilgrims. Once on land, those organisms flourished and, like water spreading through a dry sponge, they split off into divergent phyla, sub-phyla, families, orders, etc. Some of them, like the porpoise, decided to return to the sea. (Perhaps there were prophets in their midst who warned them *we* were coming, and they opted to quit land rather than deal with us.)

This propensity to judge and label ourselves and others has wreaked havoc with us and with our planet. We're only too aware of the atrocities we've visited upon one another in the name of social and religious "cleansing". We may be less aware of how much we hurt ourselves personally when we place greater value on what is outside us rather than on what is inside.

As the lights dimmed that night in our library, and the first slides of the Cape's coyotes were projected onto the screen, I thought of how foolish, and yet how tempting, it is to label and judge ourselves and others.

The coyote lives in a clearly defined hierarchy on our lovely little peninsula. They are social animals, each of them well aware of their territorial boundaries and their position within their group. This clearly defined social structure makes their lives less complicated and ensures an adequate food supply for each member within that specific territorial range.

But coyotes don't meet in libraries to attend lectures about humans for the sole purpose of learning. They don't design, build, and launch spaceships and suspend complicated telescopes above our tiny planet so that they can gaze at galaxies millions of light years away and ponder the meaning of their existence. And they don't experience the unsettling yet satisfying blend of excitement and humility that results from such endeavors.

Neither do coyotes imprison, torture, mutilate or murder one another in the name of their convictions, their creator, or the labels that they assign to one another.

Only humans do that. What a strange washashore we are. A paradoxical mixture of monster and miracle.

It may be tempting, less thought provoking, less personally demanding, to resort to labelling others, but our inherent nature as seekers of truth denies us the luxury of such limited thinking. We know too much about how little we know. Indeed, we are a most curious washashore. . . .

About the Author

Ken Brynildsen was born in 1944 in New Brunswick, New Jersey. Shortly after his birth, his family moved, and he grew up in Rye, New York. He graduated Pace University with a B.A. in English Literature. He began writing shortly after his marriage in 1976. His first novel, *School's Out!* was published by Coward, McCann and Geoghegan in 1982. In the years that followed, he had feature articles, essays, short stories and poetry published in a variety of local and regional publications.

His employment history has been both interesting and diverse. He worked for nearly 20 years as a tree surgeon in southern New York State. In 1981, he was hired by IBM, working first on a computer chip manufacturing line and later as a speechwriter and editor. He left IBM in the fall of 1988 during the company's first downsizing program. He joined his wife, Linda, as a partner in a gift business she had established in 1981.

He and Linda have two children. They live in a quiet and lovely neighborhood in Sandwich, Massachusetts, overlooking Cape Cod Bay.